THE NITTY-GRITTY
Gardening Book
FUN PROJECTS for ALL SEASONS

Kari Cornell

PHOTOGRAPHS BY
Jennifer S. Larson

M Millbrook Press · Minneapolis

For Brian, Will, and Theo,
my favorite gardening
companions
—K.C.

For Isaiah and Grace,
who love to garden
—J.S.L.

Text copyright © 2015 by Kari Cornell
Photographs copyright © 2015 by Jennifer S. Larson

Millbrook Press
A division of Lerner Publishing Group, Inc.
241 First Avenue North
Minneapolis, MN 55401 USA

For reading levels and more information, look up this title at www.lernerbooks.com.

Additional images are used with the permission of: © iStockphoto.com/AntiMartina (sunflower seeds and pumpkin seeds); USDA Plant Hardiness Zone Map, 2012. Agricultural Research Service, U.S. Department of Agriculture. Accessed from http://planthardiness.ars.usda.gov, p. 8; © Alexey Antipov/Dreamstime.com, p. 41 (bottom left). Illustrations © Laura Westlund/Independent Picture Service.

Main body text set in Frutiger LT Pro 11/15.
Typeface provided by Linotype AG.

Library of Congress Cataloging-in-Publication Data

Cornell, Kari A.
    The nitty-gritty gardening book: fun projects for all seasons / Kari Cornell ; photography by Jennifer S. Larson.
        pages   cm
    Includes index.
    ISBN 978-1-4677-2647-4 (lib. bdg. : alk. paper)
    ISBN 978-1-4677-6301-1 (EB pdf)
    1. Gardening—Juvenile literature. 2. Gardening for children. I. Larson, Jennifer S., 1967– , photographer. II. Title.
SB457.C66 2015
635.083—dc23   2014009384

Manufactured in the United States of America
1 – CG – 12/31/2014

Table of Contents

Introduction

Why Garden?

If you've ever eaten a just-picked cherry tomato, still warm from the sun, you know one of the answers to this question. Fresh fruits and vegetables taste amazing. Snap peas, carrots, and radishes are crunchy and crisp. Tomatoes and strawberries are loaded with sweet flavor. Lettuce is delicate and delicious.

When you grow your own food, you know exactly what those plants, fruits, and vegetables have been through during the growing season. You know, for example, that the plants were grown in good, healthy soil. You know that you gave them enough water and treated the plants with care. Best of all, you know that you helped grow them. How cool is that?

Gardening for the Earth

Of course there's more to gardening than growing vegetables. Colorful flowers in bloom help make your home or yard a more inviting place to play and relax. And if you fill your yard with flowering plants that are native to your area, you're helping the local ecosystem—the plants, the soil, the insects, and the birds in an area that all support one another. An ecosystem is like a jigsaw puzzle. When one or more of the pieces are missing or out of place, it affects the other pieces of the puzzle as well.

In the garden, insects such as honeybees, butterflies, and ladybugs are key pieces of the ecosystem puzzle. Bees spread pollen from one flower to the next. This is called pollination, and the flowers that bloom on fruit and vegetable plants rely on it. The female part of the plant takes in the pollen to make the seeds that will eventually grow into a berry, a squash, a tomato, or another tasty treat. Butterflies also spread pollen as they travel from flower to flower. And ladybugs help by eating insects such as aphids that can harm plants.

So by planting a garden in your yard or growing a few plants in pots on your patio, you're being good to the planet! And when you're tending to plants outside, remember that most insects you see are doing good work. Watch your plants carefully, and you will begin to see how everything within an ecosystem works together—the sun, the rain, the wildlife, and even the soil.

Gardening Basics

Ready to get started? First, you'll need to gather information about your space and do some planning. Then make sure you have the tools and the supplies you'll need.

Evaluate Your Garden Space

Do you have room to plant a garden in your yard? Or would it be better to grow plants in pots? Talk to an adult about what works best for your space.

NATIVE PLANTS

Some of the projects in this book let you pick from several types of plants or seeds. Here's a way to choose: Are some of the plants native to your area? Those would be great options.

Native plants are used to the soil, amount of rain, and climate (average weather conditions) where you live. They usually don't need as much water as nonnative plants do. And that means you can use less water on your garden during the hot summer months.

Native plants are also used to the insects, the wildlife, and other plants that thrive in your part of the world. They're good for your neighborhood and for the globe!

Planting your own garden in a corner of the yard is great, but if you only have space on a balcony or even a windowsill, you can still have fun with gardening and do many of the projects in this book.

If you do decide to plant in your yard, ask an adult to help you dig. Always call the local diggers hotline before you dig. Someone will come to your yard and mark all buried utility lines (power, water, sewer, gas, cable) so you can avoid them while digging. Also, be sure to test your soil by following the instructions here.

Test Your Soil

For some projects in this book—including the Birds and Bees Garden and the Sweet Pea or Pole Bean Tent—you will grow plants in the ground around your home. Anytime you plant in the ground, test your soil first. Soil pH is a measure of chemicals that make up the soil. The chemicals in the soil affect how easily plants can take in nutrients from the earth. Knowing the pH of your soil helps you select plants that will grow well in it.

Some plants, such as blueberries, strawberries, hydrangea, and bleeding heart, grow best in acidic soil (pH of 4.0 to 6.5). Sunflowers, peonies, and other plants do well in alkaline soil (pH of 7.0 to 7.5). Many vegetables, such as lettuce, peas, cucumbers, and carrots, prefer a pH somewhere in the middle (pH of 6.0 to 7.0). That's called neutral soil.

Easy-to-use soil testing kits can be found at your local garden or hardware store. Have an adult help you follow the directions on the package to test a small sample of your soil. What if the test results show that your soil is too acidic or too alkaline for what you plan to grow? Talk to workers at a garden center to find out how to make the soil more or less acidic by adding things like cocoa hulls, compost, or peat moss. This is called amending the soil.

Map the Sunlight

Many plants, especially those that produce fruits and vegetables, need lots of sunshine. Whether you are starting seeds or planting seedlings from a garden store, be sure to check the seed packet or plant tag to see how many hours per day of sunlight the plant will need to grow.

To see just how much sunlight your plants receive, watch over your garden for a day. If you discover you love to garden, you may even want to track the sun in different seasons. On a sunny day, take a picture of your garden (or wherever you plan to put container plants) at different times throughout the day. Snap a picture of your space at 8 a.m., 10 a.m., 12 p.m., 2 p.m., 4 p.m., and 6 p.m.

Look at the photos and notice where the sunniest spots are in your garden. Are some areas in the shade in the morning but in full sun by afternoon? Do all parts of the garden receive the same amount of sun? If not, divide the garden into sections according to the amount of sunlight received. Print your photos and line them up in the order that you took them. Count the number of hours that different parts of your

garden are in the sun. Select one of the photos, and on each area of the garden, write down the number of hours that spot is in the sun.

Knowing how much sun each area receives will make it easier to choose plants for your garden. If you try to grow a sun-loving plant in an area that only receives a couple of hours of morning sun, the plant may not flower or produce fruit.

8:00 a.m.

2:00 p.m.

Know Your Zone!

Did you know that there are many different growing zones in the United States? Each plant hardiness zone has different growing conditions, which include the amount of rain that falls in a year and how warm or cold it gets. Together, these conditions are called climate. Look at the zone map on page 8 and find the zone in which you live. When planning a garden and buying plants, look for plants that are able to grow in your particular zone. For example, if you live in zone 4 but you buy plants that grow well in zone 8, your plants will likely die unless you bring them inside during the colder months. Paying close attention to zone will make your first attempts at gardening happier for you and your plants.

Watering and Feeding Your Plants

Your plants need water and "food," just like you. Be sure to water inside plants once or twice each week. If your garden is outside, water plants using a watering can or hose every day that it doesn't rain.

Use good detective work to see which plants need water. First, check the soil. Stick your finger about an inch into the soil to see if it is moist. If it is dry, give the plants some water. Second, look at the plants. Some plants will wilt when they are thirsty. Give them a drink! Keep in mind that plants in the ground won't dry out as quickly as plants that are in pots or planters. This is because the roots of plants in a garden can pull moisture from surrounding soil.

Plants need food too. Some of the projects in this book call for compost. Compost is a mixture of decayed food scraps, plants, and soil that

DRAW A SUN MAP

You can create a sun map of your garden without a camera as well. You'll need a piece of paper, a pencil, and six colored pencils. Draw a picture of your garden area. Include fences, buildings, pathways and other items that help define your garden space. Check your garden at 8 a.m., 10 a.m., 12 p.m., 2 p.m., 4 p.m., and 6 p.m. Notice the spots that remain in the sun and those that are shady at different times of the day. Each time you check it, use a different colored pencil to lightly color in the sunny areas of your garden. Count the number of hours the different parts of your garden receive sun. Write these numbers down on your map.

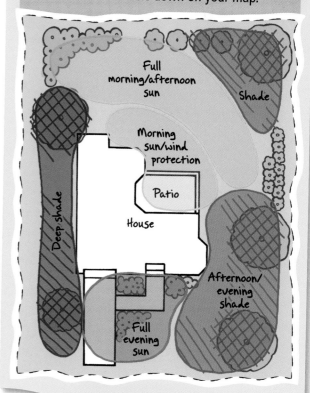

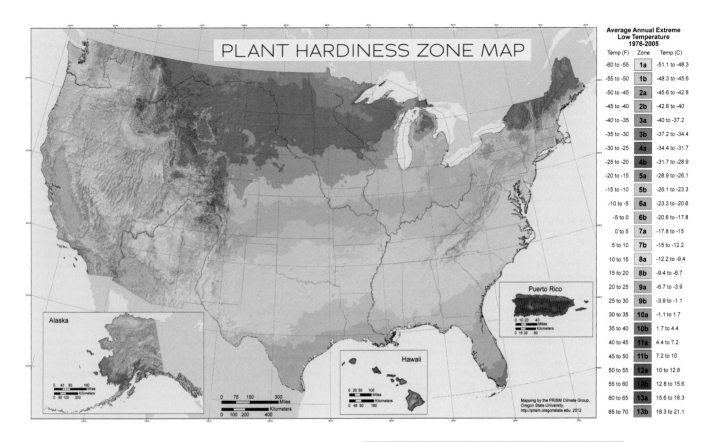

PLANT HARDINESS ZONE MAP

Average Annual Extreme Low Temperature 1976-2005

Temp (F)	Zone	Temp (C)
-60 to -55	1a	-51.1 to -48.3
-55 to -50	1b	-48.3 to -45.6
-50 to -45	2a	-45.6 to -42.8
-45 to -40	2b	-42.8 to -40
-40 to -35	3a	-40 to -37.2
-35 to -30	3b	-37.2 to -34.4
-30 to -25	4a	-34.4 to -31.7
-25 to -20	4b	-31.7 to -28.9
-20 to -15	5a	-28.9 to -26.1
-15 to -10	5b	-26.1 to -23.3
-10 to -5	6a	-23.3 to -20.6
-5 to 0	6b	-20.6 to -17.8
0 to 5	7a	-17.8 to -15
5 to 10	7b	-15 to -12.2
10 to 15	8a	-12.2 to -9.4
15 to 20	8b	-9.4 to -6.7
20 to 25	9a	-6.7 to -3.9
25 to 30	9b	-3.9 to -1.1
30 to 35	10a	-1.1 to 1.7
35 to 40	10b	1.7 to 4.4
40 to 45	11a	4.4 to 7.2
45 to 50	11b	7.2 to 10
50 to 55	12a	10 to 12.8
55 to 60	12b	12.8 to 15.6
60 to 65	13a	15.6 to 18.3
65 to 70	13b	18.3 to 21.1

Alaska

Puerto Rico

Hawaii

Mapping by the PRISM Climate Group, Oregon State University. http://prism.oregonstate.edu. 2012

adds nutrients and helps new plants to grow. It's available in bags at garden stores, or you can make it yourself by following the directions to Make a Compost Bin on page 36. It's always a good idea to work some compost into the soil when you are planting a new garden. Mixing a little compost in with potting soil is also good for potted plants.

Tending the Garden

As your garden grows, be sure to visit your plants each day. Do they look healthy? Do they need water? Does a tomato plant or an unruly vine need to be tied to a stake for support? Clip off any flower blooms that have turned dry and brown, snip off any brown leaves, and keep your garden tidy.

Tools and Supplies

What do you need to get started? A few of the basic tools and supplies you will need to do any kind of gardening project are shown on page 9. Most of the projects in this book require at least a few of these items. Be sure to check out the You Will Need list for each project before you begin. If you have trouble finding a tool or an item, see the list of Where to Find Supplies on page 47.

Before You Begin

Talk to your mom, dad, or another adult at home about the project you plan to do and make sure they approve of your plan. It would be disappointing to start a project only to discover

spade

hoe

garden gloves

watering can

trowel

compost

potting soil

terra-cotta or plastic pots

that your mom had another idea for that same patch of soil.

Before you begin a project, carefully read through all the instructions for the project you plan to make. Find out what tools and supplies you'll need. Gather the supplies you already have and make a list of those items you'll need to buy.

Set up a place to work. Projects for spring, summer, and fall can be done outside at a table or in a corner of the yard. If you sometimes eat at the table, be sure to cover it with newspaper, plastic, or a small tarp. For the winter projects, check with an adult about the best place to work inside.

Wear clothes that are OK to get dirty. Old jeans, a long-sleeved T-shirt, socks and tennis shoes, and a hat are great for gardening. Covering your skin will keep the bugs from biting, and a hat will shade your head and prevent sunburn. Use sunscreen on any skin that's not covered. And don't forget your gardening gloves! These are usually made of leather or heavy cloth and are designed to protect your hands from thorns, rocks, or tough plant stems. Find a pair in your size at your local gardening center or hardware store.

Lastly, get set to wait! It may take weeks or months to see your plants growing after you plant seeds or start a project. Keep watering and caring for the plants, and be patient. Get excited for the flowers or the fruits and veggies that are in store for later!

SPRING

THIS IS THE BUSIEST TIME OF YEAR IN THE GARDEN. The bright green tips of crocus bulbs push their way through the soil. And when the nights are above freezing, flowers and vegetables can be planted outside in window boxes and pots. So let's roll up our sleeves and get growing!

Start Your Own Seeds

Spring is on its way, but it's not quite here yet. Planting some seeds indoors might be just the thing to cure cabin fever! We'll plant sunflower seeds in this project, but feel free to plant any seeds that could use a head start—tomatoes, peppers, pumpkin, cucumber, zucchini, cosmos, or zinnias all work well as seedlings.

You will need:

small pots (either newspaper pots—made from old newspaper, 1 16-ounce [453-gram] can, and tape—or plastic or paper disposable cups or seedling pots)

gardening gloves

a trowel

1 bag potting soil

1 packet of seeds

a pen

1 Popsicle stick for each pot

a spray bottle

a waterproof tray, large enough to hold the pots

a plastic thermometer

Making Newspaper Pots

Handmade pots are great, because you can place the whole thing into the ground at planting time. The measurements here are for a newspaper about 12 inches (30 centimeters) wide by about 22 inches (56 cm) long, but a newspaper of a slightly different size is OK. If you're using other pots, skip to Planting the Seeds.

1. Open a two-page spread of the newspaper on the table in front of you. Carefully rip the page in half, right down the center-fold line. You will have two pages, each measuring about 22 by 12 inches (56 by 30.5 cm). Set aside one half.

2. Fold the sheet in half from top to bottom and then fold in half again from left to right. Your folded sheet of paper should measure 11 by 6 inches (28 by 15 cm).

3. Position the folded sheet vertically in front of you with the fold line on the right. Place the can horizontally across the fold and about 1 inch (2.5 cm) from the bottom of the page. The top 1 inch of the can should be to the right of the folded edge.

4. Lift the bottom of the page to meet the side of the can and hold it there while you roll the can and paper up to the top of the page.

5. Use two pieces of tape to hold the seam.

6. Press the excess paper on the left side against the bottom of the can and use a couple of pieces of tape to secure it. Place the can right side up, and gently tap the bottom of the can on the tabletop to flatten the paper against the can.

7. Slide the paper pot off the can.

8. Repeat steps 2 through 7 to make as many pots as you'd like.

Planting the Seeds

1. Cover your worktable with heavy plastic or an old sheet (something that's OK to get dirty).

2. Use the trowel to fill each pot with dirt. Tap pots on the table to settle the dirt, making sure there is a 1-inch (2.5 cm) gap between the top of the pot and the surface of the soil.

3. In the center of each pot, poke your index finger into the soil down to your first knuckle.

4. Drop three seeds into each hole and cover over with dirt.

5. Use the pen to label a Popsicle stick for each pot. Write the type of seed you planted and the date on one end. Push a labeled stick into each pot.

6. Use the spray bottle to moisten the soil in each pot. Place the seedling pots on the tray in front of a bright, sunny window to sprout.

7. Spray seedlings each day to keep the soil moist. Sprouts should break through the surface of the soil in 7 to 10 days.

8. Plan to transplant the seedlings into the garden outside when the soil warms to between 50°F and 70°F (10°C and 21°C) and nighttime temperatures stay above 40°F (4°C).

Build a Sweet Pea or Pole Bean Tent

This is a fun garden project that can be as large or small as you'd like it, depending on the space you have. If you have a large area, consider building a tent that's big enough to use for your own little hideout!

1. Clear a space in your garden for the tent, pulling weeds and using a garden hoe to break up the top 3 inches (7.5 cm) of the soil.

2. Ask an adult to help you arrange the gardening stakes or twigs with one end down to form a circle at least 1.5 feet (0.5 m) across, keeping a distance of about 6 inches (15 cm) between each. If you plan to use the tent as a hideout, make sure the circle formed by the stakes creates a space large enough for you to sit, about 3 feet (0.9 m) across. And remember to leave a wider opening between two stakes as a doorway!

You will need:

gardening gloves

a garden hoe

6 to 8 bamboo 5-foot (1.5 m) gardening stakes or gathered sturdy twigs

a ruler, a tape measure, or a yardstick

a hammer

scissors

1 roll of twine

a trowel

1 package sweet pea or pole bean seeds

a watering can

3. Push each stake about 4 inches (10 cm) into the ground, using a hammer to pound it in if needed.

4. Use the scissors to cut a piece of twine 24 inches (61 cm) long. Pull together the tops of the stakes and ask an adult to hold them for you. About 6 inches (15 cm) from the top, wrap the twine around all the stakes one time and tie a double knot to hold the stakes together. Continue to wrap twine around all the stakes, laying the next round of twine just below the one above, working your way down until you have just enough twine left to tie another double knot.

5. Give your bean or pea vines something to hang on to by wrapping the tent frame with twine. The twine will act as rungs on a ladder, giving the vines a place to climb. First, unwrap about an arm's length of twine and tie the end to the bottom of one of the tent stakes using a double knot. With the twine still attached to the ball, wrap the twine tightly around each stake of the tent. Work your way up the tent as you wrap around it three times. You should have three "rungs."

When you reach the top, tie the twine around one of the stakes using a double knot. (If you want to be able to go in and out, leave the space between two stakes open.)

6. To plant the beans or the peas, use a trowel to form a circle in the dirt around the outside of the stakes.

7. Read the instructions on the back of the seed packet to determine how deep to plant the seeds and how far apart to space them. If needed, use the trowel to make the circle a little deeper (beans and peas are usually planted 0.5 inch [1.25 cm] deep and 1 to 2 inches [2.5 to 5 cm] apart).

8. Use a scissors to cut open the top of the seed packet. Take care not to cut the instructions on the back, as you might want to reread them later on. Sprinkle a few seeds into your hand and drop them one by one into the circle, spacing the seeds as the instructions say. Repeat until you've planted seeds all around the stakes. Use the trowel

to cover the seeds with dirt. Then pat the dirt down firmly with the palm of your hand.

9. Use a watering can to water your seeds. Keep the planted area damp over the next several days as you watch for the tiny green seedlings to appear. As the plants grow and climb, guide them to the twine rungs on your tent. Before long, the tent will be covered in green leaves, then flowers, and then beans or peas!

Grow a Sack of Potatoes

This is a fun way to grow potatoes that doesn't require a lot of room. In fact, these bags will work just as well in a sunny corner of your yard or on a small balcony. Potatoes don't do well in hot weather, so be sure to plant in early spring, when the nights are still cool and daytime temperatures are in the 60s°F (15°C to 20°C).

a paring knife

3 seedling potatoes (small potatoes used to grow potato plants) or organic potatoes

1 burlap sack or other bag, 2 feet (0.6 m) wide and 4 feet (1.2 m) tall

scissors

gardening gloves

3 bags potting soil

1 bag compost

a trowel

a watering can

a cardboard box

a paper bag

NO BURLAP BAG? NO PROBLEM!

If you don't have a burlap bag, the potatoes can be grown in the potting soil bag itself. Simply open the bag and scoop two-thirds of the soil into a big pot or pail. Set the pot or the pail aside for later use. Roll back the sides of the bag until they are about 2 inches (5 cm) above the surface of the soil. Use a utility knife to slice a few small slits along the bottom and sides of the bag for drainage. (Holes should not be so big that the soil drains out.) Plant seedling potatoes according to directions.

1. Ask an adult to help you cut potato seedlings or organic potatoes into 2-inch (5 cm) pieces, making sure each piece has one or two "eyes." Allow potatoes to sit on a counter or a cooling rack, cut side exposed, at room temperature for a few days until the cut ends dry out (to prevent the ends from rotting). It's fine if the potato eyes start to grow shoots while the cut sides dry.

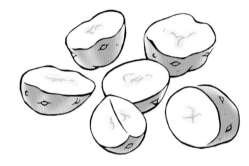

2. When you are ready to plant, gather all the tools and supplies you will need. Place the bag in the area of the yard or patio where you'll be growing the potatoes. Along the outside of the burlap bag, roll down the edges to create a container that is about 10 inches (25 cm) tall.

3. Use a scissors to open the bags of potting soil and compost as you need them. Use the trowel to fill the burlap bag with about 8 inches (20 cm) of soil. Add a couple of scoops of compost and mix the compost into the soil with the trowel.

4. Place the trimmed potato seedlings or organic potatoes into the soil, spaced about 4 inches (10 cm) apart, with eyes facing up. Push the potatoes 2 inches (5 cm) into the soil and cover with a layer of compost.

5. Water the top of the soil lightly, keeping the soil moist but not too wet.

6. Each day, check the soil to see if the seedlings need watering. Be sure to keep the soil moist. You should begin to see seedlings push through the soil in two to three weeks. If you don't see any plants by that time, carefully remove the soil from above the seedlings and check to see if they've sprouted. Replace any that have not sprouted with new potato seedlings.

7. When the plants have grown to a height of 2 to 3 inches (5 to 7.5 cm), use a trowel to carefully add more potting soil. Mound the soil around the stems, leaving the leaves untouched.

8. Continue to watch your plants, adding extra potting soil when the stems extend another 2 inches (5 cm) above the soil. Roll up the sides of the bag as needed to provide more room for the soil.

9. Blossoms on the potato plants are a sign that you have potatoes under the soil. Allow the plants to grow until the leaves and stems wilt and turn brown. (For most types of potatoes, this will take about 90 days.)

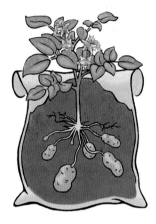

FAST-GROWING POTATOES

Here are a few reliable, fast-growing types of potatoes. Check with your local gardening center for other varieties that thrive in your area.

DESIREE

YUKON GOLD

PURPLE VIKING

10. To harvest the potatoes, use a trowel to carefully break up the soil a few inches from the stems of the plants. Use your hands to check the turned-up soil for potatoes. Place potatoes in a cardboard box.

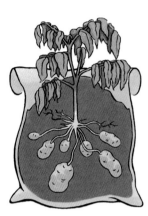

11. Empty the soil from the potato bag into your compost or ask an adult to help you spread it on the garden. Put away your tools and supplies.

12. Arrange the potatoes in a single layer along the bottom of the box. Store the box in a cool, dark, dry place for a couple of weeks. This allows the potatoes to cure, or dry out.

13. After the potatoes have cured, move them to a paper bag; close the bag; and store it in a dark, cool, dry place until ready to use. Dust off dirt and scrub well with a vegetable brush and cool, clean water before eating.

SUMMER

IN THE HEIGHT OF THE SUMMER SEASON, PLANTS OF ALL KINDS GROW LIKE CRAZY.

LONGER DAYLIGHT HOURS MEAN A PLANT'S LEAVES SPEND THE DAYS SOAKING UP SUNLIGHT AND TRANSFORMING THOSE BRIGHT RAYS INTO THE FOOD THEY NEED TO GROW. This is when daylilies burst open with vibrant color. Pole beans and sweet peas climb an inch a day. Tomatoes and pepper plants begin to form the tiny buds and flowers that will hold fruit later in the season.

Spend these warmer days on your patio or in the garden. Check on your plants each day to make sure they have enough water. If it looks as if a plant is growing so much it can no longer hold up its branches, have an adult help you support the plant with a few bamboo stakes and cloth ties or a store-bought tomato cage. Carefully remove any dried flowers or leaves. Most of all, take time to enjoy this colorful time in the garden!

Plant a Strawberry Basket

Strawberry plants spread easily, so gardeners often plant them in pots to keep them contained. Planting them in a basket can be fun too. Be sure to use a basket that's OK to get dirty and worn.

scissors

1 tall kitchen garbage bag (13 gallons, or 49 liters)

1 basket at least 8 inches (20 cm) deep and 12 inches (30 cm) wide

gardening gloves

a trowel

1 bag potting soil

1 bag compost or 2 scoops of homemade compost

2 or 3 strawberry plants

a watering can

1. Use a scissors to snip about 12 slits along the bottom 4 inches (10 cm) of the tall kitchen garbage bag, making each slit 1 inch (2.5 cm) long. Place slits randomly along the bag, working your way from the bottom.

2. Place the bag in the basket and press the sides of the bag against the inside walls of the basket. Roll the top of the bag out to cover the top edge of the basket.

3. Use a trowel to fill the basket with potting soil. Stop when the soil level is about 3 inches (7.5 cm) below the top of the basket.

4. Add two scoops of compost and use the trowel to mix the compost evenly into the potting soil.

5. Plan where you will put each plant so the plants are spaced 6 inches (15 cm) apart. Dig a hole in the soil 2 inches (5 cm) deep and insert the first strawberry plant. To remove the plant from its plastic pot, squeeze the bottom of the pot to loosen the soil. Then cover the top of the pot with one hand as you tip the pot upside down with the other. You may have to squeeze the pot again to release the plant and roots. Gently tuck the plant into the hole with roots down. Use the trowel to add dirt to fill the hole. Then press firmly around the plant to secure it.

6. Repeat step 5 to plant the remaining strawberry plants.

7. Use a scissors to trim the liner bag right along the top of the soil line.

8. Use a watering can to water the strawberry plants. Water each day in warm weather. Harvest strawberries when red and soft.

Make a Birds and Bees Garden

Flowers, fruit trees, and vegetable plants need a little help from the birds, the bees, and the butterflies. These animals help plants reproduce by spreading pollen from one plant to another. You can help attract these pollinators to your yard by planting certain flowers in your garden. Ask at your local garden store about varieties that work well in your area, or visit the Lady Bird Johnson Wildflower Center website (listed on page 46) for local plant ideas. If you don't have space to plant in the ground, a container garden works just as well.

Ask an adult to help you decide whether to plant a garden in the ground or in pots and other containers. Remember that flowering plants need at least six hours of sun each day, so pick a sunny spot for your garden.

You will need:

3 or 4 of these types of plants or seeds:

> brown-eyed Susan
>
> cosmos
>
> delphinium
>
> dianthus
>
> petunias
>
> phlox
>
> pink coneflower
>
> yarrow
>
> zinnia

several terra-cotta pots in various sizes, for a container garden only

a spade and a hoe, for planting in the ground

a trowel

compost

potting soil, for a container garden only

a watering saucer to fit under a 12-inch (30 cm) terra-cotta pot

a 6-inch (15 cm) pot for a birdbath stand

small stones

mulch (material to cover the ground around plants, such as straw or wood chips)

a watering can

1. Ask an adult to help you prepare the soil. To plant in an existing garden, use a hoe to scratch up the soil to make it nice and loose. Then skip to step 5.

2. To create a new garden, use the trowel to "trace" the outline of the garden in the grass, like you would use a pencil to draw a shape on a piece of paper.

3. Use the trowel or a spade to lift the layer of grass from the new garden space. While standing over the space, shake as much dirt from the grass as possible. Place the grass in a yard waste bag or in your outside compost bin, if you have one.

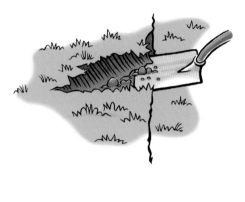

4. Now "double dig" the soil. To double dig, you'll push the spade all the way down into the dirt to mix the soil two times. First, insert the tip of the spade into the soil. Then place one foot on the top of the shovel blade and use your weight to push it into the ground. When your feet come close to the ground, turn the shovelful of dirt over onto the garden, and insert the spade again into the same spot. Again, push the shovel all the way into the ground, pull it out, and turn the dirt onto the garden. Repeat this every 6 inches (15 cm) around your garden space to break up the soil.

5. Use a hoe to mix a bag of compost into the soil before adding plants.

6. Plan your garden. Figure out where you would like to place plants and where you might scatter seeds. Read plant tags and seed packets to see how big the plants will grow and how far apart to space them. Be sure to place taller plants in the center or back of the garden and shorter plants toward the edges or front of the garden. Also leave room to set up a small birdbath, made from the watering saucer and a 6-inch (15 cm) terra-cotta pot.

7. Use the trowel to dig holes for your plants, following the directions on the plant tag. To remove the plant from its plastic pot, squeeze the bottom of the pot to loosen the soil. Then cover the top of the pot with one hand as you tip the pot upside down with the other. You may have to squeeze the pot again to release the plant and roots. Gently tuck the plant into the hole with roots down. Use a trowel to add dirt to fill the hole. Then press firmly around the plant to secure it.

8. Follow the directions on seed packets to plant seeds.

9. Give your new garden a drink by watering it with a watering can or a hose on the "mist" setting. Water it every day that it doesn't rain.

Making a Container Butterfly Garden

1. Arrange your pots on your patio or other gardening space. Plant seeds in some of the pots by filling the pots to 2 inches (5 cm) below the rim with potting soil. Follow the directions on the back of each seed packet to sow the seeds.

2. To plant plants, fill each pot halfway with potting soil.

3. To remove a plant from its plastic pot, squeeze the bottom of the pot to loosen the soil. Then cover the top of the pot with one hand as you tip the pot upside down with the other. You may have to squeeze the pot again to release the plant and roots.

4. Gently tuck the plant into the hole with roots down. Use a trowel to add dirt to fill the hole. Then press firmly around the plant to secure it.

5. Repeat steps 3 and 4 to put the remaining plants in pots.

6. Water the plants with a watering can or a hose on the "mist" setting. Water them every day that it doesn't rain.

Setting Up a Birdbath

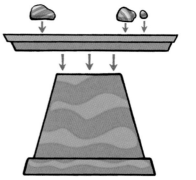

1. Place the 6-inch (15 cm) pot upside down on a level surface in or near your garden. Center the watering tray, edges up, on top of the upside-down pot.

2. Add pebbles to the tray for decoration.

3. With a watering can or a garden hose, fill the birdbath with fresh, clean water. Then make sure to keep it full!

Create a Hanging Garden

If you don't have a lot of space for a garden but you want to grow your own veggies, this is the project for you. Simply hang your vegetable garden over a balcony or plant it in a large pot on a patio.

You will need:

gardening gloves

a trowel

1 hanging basket with a hanger, or a large pot, at least 12 inches (30 cm) wide

1 bag potting soil

1 bag compost

1 thyme plant

1 chive plant

1 cherry tomato plant (small seedling size)

1 Swiss chard plant

scissors

1 packet lettuce seeds

1 packet nasturtium seeds

a watering can

1. Use a trowel to fill the hanging basket or a large pot with potting soil. Fill to about 2 inches (5 cm) below the top of the pot.

2. Add four scoops of compost, and use the trowel to mix the compost evenly into the potting soil.

3. To plant the thyme, dig a hole in the soil about 2 inches (5 cm) in from the edge of the pot and 3 to 4 inches (7.5 to 10 cm) deep. To remove the plant from its plastic pot, squeeze the bottom of the pot to loosen the soil. Then cover the top of the pot with one hand as you tip the pot upside down with the other. You may have to squeeze the pot again to release the plant and roots. Gently tuck the plant into the hole with roots down. Use a trowel to add dirt to fill the hole. Then press firmly around the plant to secure it.

4. Repeat step 3 to plant the chive plant and the cherry tomato plant along the edge of the pot. Plant the Swiss chard plant in the center of the pot. Be sure to space the plants about 4 inches (10 cm) apart, and leave a couple of areas bare for scattering the lettuce and nasturtium seeds.

5. Read the instructions on the back of the lettuce seed packet to determine how deep to plant the seeds. Use the trowel to scrape away the top ¼ to ½ inch (0.6 to 1.25 cm) of dirt from the area where you'll be scattering the seeds.

6. Cut open the top of the lettuce seed packet. Take care not to cut the instructions on the back of the packet, as you might want to reread them later on. Sprinkle a handful of seeds into your hand and scatter them into the planting area. Use the trowel to cover the seeds with dirt. Then pat the seeds down firmly with the palm of your hand.

7. Repeat steps 5 and 6 with the nasturtium seeds.

8. Use a watering can to water your seeds and the other plants in the pot. Keep the planted areas damp over the next several days as you watch for the tiny green seedlings to appear.

9. Hang your basket or place your pot in a sunny spot in your yard. As the plants grow, feel free to snip herbs, pick tomatoes, or harvest the lettuce to make a delicious salad. You can eat everything planted in this basket, right down to the leaves and the blossoms on the nasturtium plant! (Note: Although nasturtium flowers are edible, most flowers are not. Check with an adult before eating any flower.)

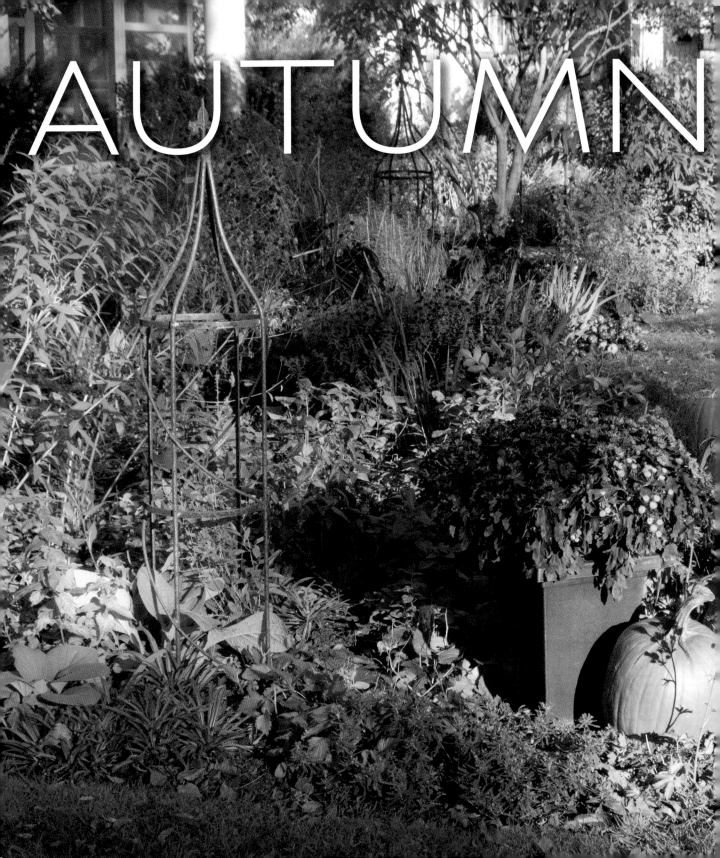

AUTUMN

THE DAYS HAVE GROWN COOLER, AND THE SUN IS SETTING EARLIER EACH DAY.

MANY PLANTS IN THE GARDEN HAVE BEGUN TO SHOW SIGNS THAT THEY ARE DONE FOR THE SEASON. In northern climates, early autumn is still a great time for vegetable gardeners. In fall's cooler temperatures, a new crop of lettuces and spinach will thrive. Pumpkins slowly turn from green to orange, and their vines begin to wither. Tomatoes seem to ripen by the minute, and root vegetables like carrots are ready to be pried from the earth. This is also the time to plant fall bulbs like daffodils, tulips, and hyacinths. Or try planting bulbs in a pot for inside blooms.

If temperatures dip below freezing where you live, keep an eye on the weather. Harvest all fruits and vegetables and cover or move all tender plants inside before the first frost.

Force a Pot of Daffodils

To "force" a pot of daffodils simply means to plant them in a pot and trick them into blooming when they wouldn't ordinarily bloom. The pot is stored in a refrigerator or other cool place for a few months. Then when the pot is placed in a warmer, sunlit room, the bulbs act as if it's springtime. They send up green shoots and eventually bloom. If you start this project in the fall, you'll have flowers blooming inside in the winter. It's a fun way to get a little spring color ahead of schedule. This project uses daffodils, but you can also try tulips, hyacinths, or paperwhites instead.

You will need:

gardening gloves

1 clean 6- to 8-inch (15 to 20 cm) clay* or plastic pot with a drainage hole and a saucer

1 small, broken clay pot, or stones that are larger than the pot's drainage hole (enough for two layers in the bottom of the pot)

a trowel

6 bulbs, with label tags saved

1 bag potting soil

a stapler

1 Popsicle stick

a pen or a pencil

a watering can

space in a refrigerator or a garage where the temperature stays around 40°F (4°C)

* If you are using a clay pot, soak the entire pot in a bucket of water for 24 hours before planting your bulbs. A dry clay pot pulls moisture from the soil. Soaking the clay pot will keep it from drying out the plant too quickly.

1. With gardening gloves on, cover the drainage hole in the bottom of the pot with pieces of the small broken clay pot or the stones.

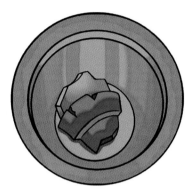

2. Use the trowel to fill the pot to within 3 inches (7.5 cm) of the rim with potting soil.

3. Add bulbs, placing them side by side with roots down and pointy tips up.

4. Add soil to cover the bottom of the bulbs, but allow the tips to stick up out of the soil. Use your fingers to press down the soil around the bulbs.

5. Staple the tag from your bulbs to a wooden Popsicle stick and label the stick with the date planted.

6. Count out 13 weeks from the current date. That's when the bulbs should be removed from cold storage. Write that date on the Popsicle stick too. Push the stick into the soil.

7. Water bulbs well, and place them in the refrigerator or other place where the temperature stays at

Planted 9/15/14
Remove from fridge 12/15/14

35°F to 45°F (2°C to 7°C). To help remember when to remove the pot of bulbs from the refrigerator, add a note on the calendar.

8. Check the bulbs a couple of times each week to make sure the soil is moist. Lightly water as needed.

9. At the end of 13 weeks, remove the bulbs from the refrigerator and place them in a sunny window. Your bulbs should shoot up green leaves and begin to bloom within three to five weeks. Once the flowers bloom, move the pot out of direct sunlight for longer-lasting blooms. Water as needed.

Create an Herb Window Box

It's fun to be able to snip a little rosemary or basil and add some summer spice to your spaghetti dinner long after the growing season has ended! With this little window box planter inside a sunny window, it's possible to grow herbs all year long.

1. Ask an adult to help you select the right window for your box of plants. Make sure the window gets lots of sun and is out of reach of pets.

2. Cover your work space with newspaper or a plastic tablecloth. Then use a trowel to fill the window box planter with potting soil. Fill to about 2 inches (5 cm) below the top of the planter.

3. Add 2 scoops compost and use the trowel to mix the compost evenly into the potting soil.

4. Decide how you'd like to arrange the herbs in the planter. Before removing the herbs from their containers, set the small pots into the planter and move them around until you like how the plants look together.

5. To plant the first herb, dig a hole in the soil about 2 inches (5 cm) in from one end of the planter and 3 to 4 inches (8 to 10 cm) deep. To remove the plant from its plastic pot, squeeze the bottom of the pot to loosen the soil. Then cover the top of the pot with one hand as you tip the pot upside down with the other. You may have to squeeze the pot again to release the plant and roots. Gently tuck the plant into the hole with roots down. Use a trowel to add dirt to fill the hole. Then press firmly around the plant to secure it.

6. Repeat step 4 to plant the rest of the herbs, digging your next hole 4 to 6 inches (10 to 15 cm) from the herb you just planted.

7. Move the planter to the windowsill.

8. Carefully water the planter, making sure water or soil doesn't flow over the edge. Keep the planter moist over the next week or so, until the plants get used to their new home. Then water once or twice a week or when the soil feels dry.

Make a Compost Bin

Many of the projects in this book call for compost, a kind of soil with lots of nutrients made from decaying fruit and vegetable scraps. You don't need a yard to make compost! With this bin that fits under the sink, you can make compost right in your kitchen. You'll just need help from some worms.

You will need:

a plastic bin with clip-on lid, small enough to fit under your sink (about 16 quarts (15 liters), or 10 inches by 16 inches (25 by 40.6 cm) and 6 inches deep (15.3 cm), or similar size)

a hammer

a small nail

sheets of newspaper, ripped into strips

a trowel

1 bag potting soil

food scraps

1 container red worms, 500 count*

a spray bottle, filled with water

* You can buy worms at your local garden store or online. See the Garden Resources section on page 46 for website listings.

1. Place the top on the plastic bin and use the hammer and the nail to pound 12 to 15 holes into the top of the lid. Holes should be no wider than ⅛ inch (0.3 cm).

2. Open the bin and add a layer of newspaper strips. Then use the trowel to add four scoops of potting soil. If you have any fruit or vegetable scraps, add them now, using the trowel to stir them into the soil and newspaper scraps. Now add those hungry worms and let them do their work! Worms like darkness, so snap on the lid and place the bin under the sink (or wherever you've decided to store it).

3. Place the trowel and a few sheets of newspaper near

the bin. If there's room, store the bag of potting soil near the bin as well.

4. Before adding fruit or vegetable scraps to the bin, be sure the pieces are smaller than 2 inches (5 cm) across. The smaller the pieces, the faster they will break down. Then carefully stir the contents of the bin with the trowel. Replace the lid and let the worms eat.

5. Keep an eye on the bin. Food scraps release moisture as they break down. Worms like moist soil, but they don't like to swim. If puddles form or the soil seems heavy with moisture, add newspaper strips and a scoop of soil to absorb the water. Stir with the trowel. If the soil seems too dry, spray the bin well with water and close the lid tightly.

6. Food scraps should break down in about three to four weeks. To use your compost, push all food scraps to one side of the bin, leaving the soil that's already broken down, and keep the other side food-free for three days. (If you have any new scraps during this time, add them to the "food side" of the bin). The worms will move to the side where you've placed the food. When the cleared side is free of worms, use the trowel to remove the compost from that side and place it in a bucket. Spread the worm-filled compost throughout the bin. Add the finished compost to your outside gardens or add to some of your container gardens.

WHAT TO FEED (AND NOT TO FEED) THE WORMS

Worms love to eat your food scraps, but there are a few foods that you should NOT add to the bin. Some scraps simply won't break down quickly enough. Other food scraps should never be added to the bin because they may harm the worms or they may smell terrible while they are decaying.

NEVER ADD THESE:
citrus fruit and peels
stems from squashes or pumpkins
large pieces of melon rinds
meat
dairy products
animal fats, such as lard
leftovers of meals that include
    meat, oils, or bones
tea bags with staples in them
egg whites or yolks

DO ADD THESE:
coffee grounds
loose tea
tea bags without staples
eggshells
small pieces of melon rind
non-citrus fruit scraps
vegetable scraps,
    cut into 2-inch (5 cm) pieces

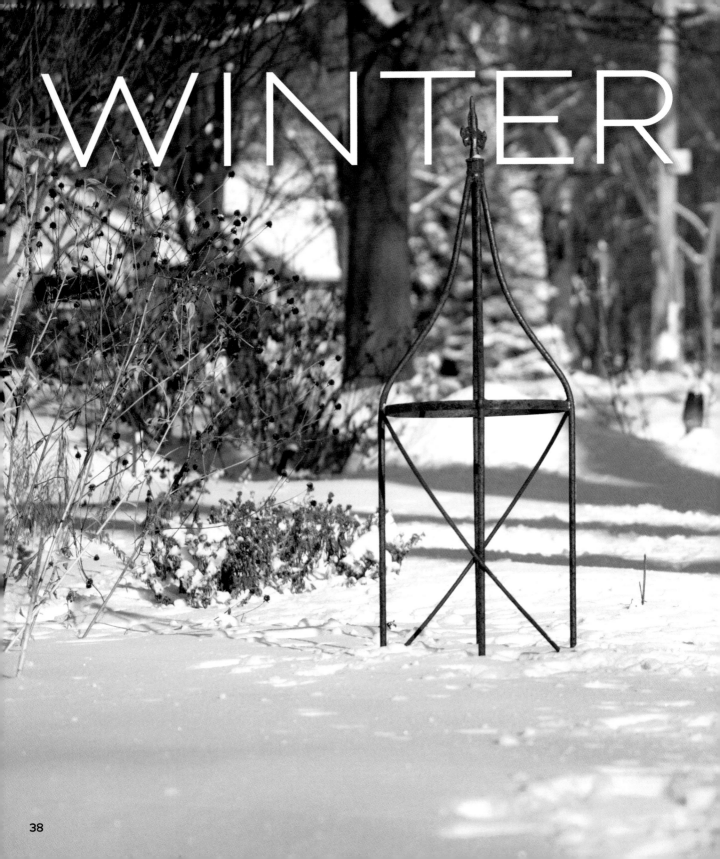

WINTER

IT MAY SEEM AS IF WINTER IS A TIME TO SET ASIDE ALL THOUGHTS OF GARDENING—ESPECIALLY IF YOU LIVE SOMEWHERE SNOWY.

BUT THERE IS NO BETTER TIME TO BEGIN DREAMING ABOUT WARMER GARDENING DAYS TO COME. Think about what seeds you might be able to start indoors for the upcoming gardening season. Sprinkle a package of mixed lettuce seeds into a pot of soil and enjoy fresh salad greens during the coldest months of the year. Sprout an avocado pit and watch it grow into a sturdy avocado plant. Or build your own terrarium, a self-contained garden that won't be affected by the elements. In this section, you'll find a few good reasons for getting your hands dirty through the winter months.

Build a Terrarium in a Jar

A terrarium is a mini-garden in a covered jar. Much like a greenhouse, the jar retains warmth and moisture, providing the perfect little ecosystem for plants to grow. Look for terrarium plants—such as ferns and others that love moisture—at your local garden store, or order some online. Be creative! Add tiny rocks, build a ladder out of sticks, or use tiny gnomes or animal figurines to decorate your jar.

You will need:

1 wide-mouthed jar, at least 5 inches (12.5 cm) tall, with a lid

a dish brush or a piece of steel wool

1-cup measuring cup

1 to 2 cups (0.25 to 0.5 liters) aquarium gravel or pebbles

a trowel

1 bag of potting soil

a Popsicle stick (optional)

1 terrarium plant (ask at a garden center or research online to find a plant that fits the size of your jar)

moss, either from your own yard or from a gardening store

a spatula

stones, acorns, or figurines for decoration

a spray bottle filled with water

1. Wash and dry your jar. If you are using an old food jar with a label, soak it in water for an hour to soften the paper. Use a dish brush or a piece of steel wool to scrape off the label.

2. Use a measuring cup to add the gravel or pebbles to the bottom of the jar. Shake the jar slightly to level the gravel. The gravel layer should be about 1 inch (2.5 cm) thick.

3. Use a trowel to add the potting soil, creating a layer about 2 inches (5 cm) thick.

4. Poke your finger or a Popsicle stick down into the soil to create a hole for the plant.

5. To remove the plant from its plastic pot, squeeze the bottom of the pot on all sides to loosen the soil. Then cover the top of the pot with one hand as you tip the pot upside down

with the other. You may have to squeeze the pot again to release the plant and roots. Gently tuck the plant into the hole with roots down. Then add dirt to fill the hole and press firmly around the plant.

6. If you have moss growing on rocks in your own yard, ask an adult if you can transplant some of it into your jar. Use a spatula to scrape the moss from the rock or ground and carefully place it onto the soil. Press it down firmly with your fingers. You can also buy moss online or at gardening stores. Remove it from its pot following the instructions in step 5.

7. Add small stones, acorns, animal figurines, or gnomes inside the jar to decorate it.

8. Spritz plants with water and close the lid to keep the moisture inside. Place the terrarium out of direct sunlight.

9. Check on your jar every few days. If moisture is forming on the side or top of the jar, remove the lid for a few minutes to release some of the water. If the soil begins to look dry, spritz with water and cover.

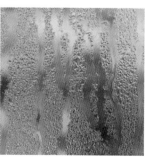

MAKE A MINI TWIG LADDER

2 thin but sturdy twigs, about 12 inches (30 cm) long

1 spread of old newspaper

a ruler

1 paper plate

white glue

1. Break one twig in half to use for the sides of the ladder and lay the halves side by side, about 1 inch (2.5 cm) apart, on the sheet of newspaper.

2. To make the rungs, or the ladder steps, break the other twig into 10 pieces, each measuring 1.5 inches (3.8 cm) long.

3. On a paper plate, squirt a puddle of white glue about the size of a quarter.

4. Dip the ends of a small twig piece into the glue and lay the rung on the ladder sides, making sure the glued edges rest against each side of the twig.

5. Repeat step 4, spacing each ladder rung about ½ inch (1.25 cm) apart, until all rungs are in place.

6. Allow the ladder to dry for a couple of hours before adding it to your terrarium.

Grow an Avocado Plant from Seed

This project takes a little patience, but is worth the effort. Watch a plant grow from the pit of a common avocado! If you want to grow your own avocados, that will take more patience and more plants. Avocado plants take at least four years to start producing fruit and need several avocado plants near one another, for pollination.

You will need:

- 1 soft, ripe avocado
- a cutting board
- a paring knife
- 4 round toothpicks
- 1 wide-mouthed glass jar
- potting soil
- a trowel
- a 6-inch (15 cm) pot with a tray
- a watering can
- a spray bottle

1. Place the avocado on its side on the cutting board and use the paring knife to cut around the entire fruit, beginning at the stem and working all the way around.

2. Twist the two sides in opposite directions to open the avocado. Remove the pit.

3. Wash the pit in cool water, rubbing away any avocado flesh with your fingers.

4. With the pit's pointed end facing down, stick four toothpicks into the pit so they stick straight out from the sides and are evenly spaced.

5. Fill the jar with water, making sure the water level is about 1 inch (2.5 cm) from the top of the jar.

6. Balance the pit on the top of the jar so that the bottom half of the pit is sitting in water.

7. Set the jar in a sunny window and allow it to sprout. This may take up to six weeks, so be patient. Change the water every five days to prevent bacteria buildup.

8. Once roots have grown from the bottom of the pit and a tiny green stem has sprouted from the top, plant the pit in soil. Use a trowel to fill the pot with 3 inches (7.5 cm) of potting soil.

9. Place the pit roots down in the soil in the center of the pot.

10. Completely cover the pit with potting soil, patting down the soil along the surface.

11. Water the pit well and place it in a sunny window to grow. As it grows taller, you may need to stake it, tying the stem to a support.

MIXED GREENS

Grow Your Own Mini Salad

With a few seeds, recycled plastic clamshell containers, and potting soil, you can transform a sunny windowsill into a mini garden. What a great way to enjoy fresh lettuce throughout the year!

You will need:

1 16-ounce (454 gram) plastic clamshell strawberry container

1 5-ounce (142 g) plastic clamshell container for greens, to use as a drainage tray

a trowel

potting soil

1 package mixed lettuce seeds

potting soil

1 package mixed lettuce seeds

a spray bottle, filled with fresh water

1. Place the strawberry container inside of the lettuce container. Use a trowel to fill the strawberry container with potting soil. Fill the container to 1 inch (2.5 cm) from the top.

2. Sprinkle half the seeds over the top of the soil. Use your fingertips to pat them down, and cover with dirt.

3. Spritz the top of the soil with water from the spray bottle, making sure the surface is very moist.

4. Place the container in a sunny spot and close the lid of the strawberry container. This will act as a little greenhouse, causing the seeds to sprout more quickly than they would if they were not covered.

5. Spritz the surface of the soil with water each day and close the lid.

6. Once seedlings sprout, open the lid. Continue to spritz each day and harvest when ready.

Glossary

amending the soil: adding things like compost or peat moss to your soil to make it more or less acidic, depending on the type of plant you want to grow

bud: a tiny plant growth in fruit and vegetable plants that will hold the fruit and vegetables once they start growing

climate: the average or typical weather conditions in a region over time

compost: a mixture of decayed food scraps, plants, and soil that is rich in nutrients

decay: when bacteria or fungi break down fruits, vegetables, dead plants, or other matter

double dig: to mix the soil twice by pushing a spade all the way down into an area of dirt two times

ecosystem: all the insects, wildlife, and other plants in an area that support and depend on one another

flower: the part of a plant where the seed or fruit grows

forcing bulbs: planting bulbs in a pot and tricking them into blooming out of season by storing in a cool place followed by a warm place

herb: a plant that is used to add flavor to food

hoe: a gardening tool with a flat blade and a long handle that can be used to pull weeds and break up soil

native plants: plants that grow naturally or have existed for many years in a given area

organic matter: decaying plant material such as compost, leaves, or grass clippings that can be added to the soil to help plants grow

pH: a measure of chemicals that make up soil that affects how easily plants can take in nutrients from the soil

plant hardiness zones: regions of the United States that have different growing conditions, including temperatures and amount of rainfall

pollination: the spreading of pollen from one flower to the next

pollinator: animals such as birds, bees, and butterflies that help plants reproduce by spreading pollen from one plant to another

seedling: a young plant

spade: a large gardening tool with a curved blade that is designed for digging into the ground

stake: a pointed stick or metal or wooden post to mark or measure out an area

trowel: a small gardening tool with a curved blade that can be used to break up soil and scoop up dirt

varieties: different types of plants that can be characterized by their appearance, the climates they grow best in, and more

Gardening Resources

Books

Bartholomew, Mel. *Square Foot Gardening with Kids: Learn Together.* Minneapolis: Cool Springs Press, 2014.

Hendy, Jenny. *Gardening Projects for Kids: Fantastic Ideas for Making Things, Growing Plants and Flowers, and Attracting Wildlife to the Garden, with 60 Practical Projects and 500 Photographs.* London: Anness, 2012.

Inciarrano, Michelle. *Tiny World Terrariums: A Step-by-Step Guide.* New York: Stewart, Tabori and Chang, 2012.

Krezel, Cindy. *Kids' Container Gardening: Year-Round Projects for Inside and Out.* Chicago: Chicago Review Press, 2010.

Lovejoy, Sharon. *Roots, Shoots, Buckets & Boots: Gardening Together with Children.* New York: Workman Publishing Company, 1999.

Pulley Sayre, April. *Touch a Butterfly: Wildlife Gardening with Kids.* Boston: Roost Books, 2013.

Tomio, Stacy. *Project Garden: A Month-by-Month Guide to Planting, Growing, and Enjoying ALL Your Backyard Has to Offer.* Avon, MA: Adams Media, 2012.

Gardening Websites

Climate Kids: NASA's Eyes on the Earth
http://climatekids.nasa.gov/mini-garden/
This website provides information on climate change and activities for kids, including ideas for making a butterfly garden and building your own terrarium.

Kid's Gardening: Helping Young Minds Grow
http://www.kidsgardening.org/
Provides resources and ideas for gardening at school and at home. Click on the Kids Garden News tab for gardening activities and tips each month.

Lady Bird Johnson Wildflower Center
http://www.wildflower.org/collections/
This site allows you to click on your state and view native plants that are recommended for your area.

National Wildlife Federation
http://www.nwf.org/How-to-Help/Garden-for-Wildlife/Gardening-Tips.aspx
The National Wildlife Federation provides a great list of gardening tips that are good for the environment, including attracting butterflies and hummingbirds, building a worm compost bin, gardening with native plants, and using less water in the garden.

The New York Botanical Garden
http://www.nybg.org/gardens/home-gardening/tips/birds-bees-butterflies.php
This website provides tips on attracting birds, bees, and butterflies to your garden. Also check out videos on how to plant your own seeds indoors and outdoors, planting potatoes, and planting strawberries.

USDA Plant Hardiness Zone Map
http://planthardiness.ars.usda.gov/PHZMWeb/
Use this map to locate your growing zone.

Where to Find Supplies
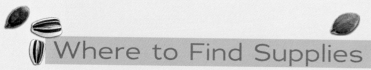

Amazon.com
Amazon is an easy, go-to source for terrarium supplies and composting worms.

Breck's
http://www.brecks.com/
Breck's is a dependable source for a wide variety of mail-order bulbs.

Bulk Apothecary
http://www.bulkapothecary.com/categories/containers /glass-apothecary-jars.html
This is a great source for all sorts of terrarium containers.

General Merchandise Stores
Target, Walmart, and other big-box stores carry seeds, pots, many terrarium container options, and other gardening supplies and tools.

Home Improvement Centers
Stores such as Home Depot, Lowes, and Menards usually have a garden center where you can find most everything you'll need for the projects in this book. Seek out native plants and organic seeds, if available.

Local Co-op Grocery Store
Many food co-ops carry organic seeds in the spring. This is also a great place to buy organic potatoes and avocados.

Local Farmers' Market
Your local farmers' market can be a great source for seeds and young plants, especially in the spring. Search for a market near you by entering your zip code at this USDA website: http://search.ams.usda.gov/ farmersmarkets/Accessible.aspx.

Local Garden Center
You'll find most everything you need at your local gardening center: seedlings, seeds, pots, tools, gardening gloves, compost, and soil. Check here for red worms and terrarium plants and supplies too. Some small, organic-focused garden stores may carry them.

Local Hardware Store
Look here for seeds, gardening tools, pots, soil, and more. Some hardware stores may sell seedlings, native plants, and vegetable plants as well.

Seed Savers Exchange
http://www.seedsavers.org/
Seed Savers Exchange is dedicated to preserving a wide variety of heirloom seeds. Look here for unique seeds that you can't find anywhere else.

Uncle Jim's Worm Farm
http://unclejimswormfarm.com/
Uncle Jim's offers a quick and easy way to buy composting worms.

Index

About the Author

Kari Cornell is a freelance writer and editor who lives with her husband and two sons in Minneapolis, Minnesota. She's a huge fan of tinkering in the garden, good food, and making something clever out of nothing. Cornell is the author of several cookbooks in the You're the Chef series from Millbrook Press and is co-author of *Growing with Purpose: Forty Years of Seward Community Cooperative*.

About the Photographer

Jennifer Larson started photographing—and gardening—when she was a kid, and she has done both ever since. Now she gardens with her own kids, tending a vegetable garden along with cherry, apple, and peach trees. This is Ms. Larson's first book as photographer. She has also written several children's nonfiction books. She lives in Minneapolis with her husband and two kids.